Simple Prayers for Complicated Lives

SIMPLE PRAYERS
for COMPLICATED LIVES

Jennifer M. Phillips

SEABURY BOOKS
an imprint of Church Publishing, Inc., New York

Library of Congress Cataloging-in-Publication Data

Phillips, Jennifer M., 1952–
    Simple prayers for complicated lives / Jennifer
Phillips.
        p.   cm.
Includes bibliographical references and index.
ISBN-13: 978-1-59627-029-9 (alk. paper)
ISBN-10: 1-59627-029-2 (alk. paper)
1. Prayers. I. Title.
BV245.P47 2006
242'.8—dc22
                            2006016042

Church Publishing, Incorporated
445 Fifth Avenue
New York, New York 10016
www.churchpublishing.org

I dedicate this book
to all those who have opened my heart
to love and have moved me to prayer,
with particular thanksgiving
for my godchildren,
J. B. Wyker,
Peter Morrow,
Christopher Gaskell,
and
Khushro and Soli Ghandhi.

CONTENTS

III. EVENING

IV. BIRTH

V. PARENTS AND CHILDREN

VI. ASSAULTS AND INTRUSIONS

VII. MIXED BLESSINGS

PREFACE

Because we are all children of the Creator, every one of us, we are all invited, entitled, and empowered to pray. I believe that God desires to hear from us, to have our thoughts, hopes, and needs expressed by us in whatever ways we can manage. For some people, prayer comes as easily as thought and speech. Others find themselves tongue-tied, uncertain, or anxious, especially in difficult situations. This book is intended to be a companion to you in your own praying and to remind you that whatever happens in your life, you may speak of it to God.

As a poet and a lover of language, I am grateful to be part of the Anglican Church, with its wonderful prayers from a long tradition of Christians to borrow and make my own. Many of the words of the *Book of Common Prayer,* along with traditions of prayer from the Bible, are etched in my memory and pop up when I need them. The custom of handing down prayers that the faithful may speak and make their own (or adapt as the occasion suggests) provides a tangible companionship for our prayer. When we hold another's words in our mouth, in our minds, we feel them praying alongside us, strengthening and encouraging us by their presence in the communion of saints. At the same time I am also aware of the limits of verbal prayer, and of the heart's need to fall into silence or groans too deep for words, as the apostle Paul put it. Sometimes I simply trust that God already knows what I would pray if I could, and the intention is enough.

Contemporary life brings complexities that have not been addressed by the prayer books of most denominations. We struggle with subjects once thought too private to mention, yet common enough that many a faithful person has struggled to find words to bring them to God: miscarriage, marital trouble, criminal victimization, employment miseries, and more. We also know and want to speak to God about ordinary joys of daily life that are perhaps not august enough to have claimed the attention of prayer book authors: sending a child to school, bringing home a new pet, buying and driving a car.

Simple Prayers for Complicated Lives

Scripture enjoins the faithful to pray without ceasing, and surely this suggests gathering even the trivial moments of our days and lifting them up to God. This little collection offers prayers for many occasions, mundane and extraordinary, for which someone might struggle for words to pray—not fancy words, nothing Elizabethan, just simple expressions that lend themselves to be spoken aloud, that are connected to the venerable tradition of Christian prayer while also fresh and direct.

Prayer is one of the ways we hold the world, ourselves, and our fellow human beings in love and appreciation. When we call a person or situation into our prayer, we are reminded that God is already present to them and to us in the midst of our experiences, even when we do not feel this to be so, even when no answer seems to come.

In particular, some of this small flock of prayers respond to challenging reproductive issues. From biblical times and likely before, women and men who have longed for a child, who have lost a child, who have feared for a child in peril have offered their anguished pleas to God, and many of us today do the same. Such prayers might seem almost too painful to read—unless you are the person who needs them.

If so, copy the ones you need and keep them handy. Tape one to your mirror. Slide one under your computer. Tuck one in your child's bookbag. Send one to a friend. If you don't find the prayer you're looking for, shape your own words, or borrow and adapt some of mine. I hope these prayers will be a blessing to you. May they draw you ever more deeply into the heart and life of the God who so loves you.

one

MORNING

AT DAWN

For first light and bird song,
I give thanks to you, Creator,
by whose hand darkness and light
were set apart, and whose imagination
dreamed this universe and breathed its life
by your enkindling Spirit and good Word.
Bless this new day and me, Lover of Souls,
to whom I give glory, honor, love, and praise.

FOR THE JOY OF THE HOUSE

God, who made the universe for your delight:
　　preserve the joy of this house.
Keep all the household in peace and contentment.
Bless our labor and our rest,
　　our solitude and our companionship.
Keep the hearth warm,
　　the door open in welcome,
　　the cupboard well-stocked,
　　and the beds comfy,
that all who enjoy home in this place
may feel your love.

STIFF BODY PRAYER

God my center and strength in pain:
lift me up today when I can hardly lift myself.

Give me perseverance
to stretch and move against resistance,
to have the same toughness of body
    as I would have of mind,
and to remain undefeated
by the difficulties of flesh and bone.

Give me courage to move
in order to stay in motion,
to keep the good humor that pain chips away,
and to celebrate the strength, the mobility,
    the gifts that I have,
rather than to count my losses and limitations.

Let your grace be fluid and lively in me
though my joints are stiff and sore,
and let me have that mind which was in Christ,
who did not measure his own suffering,
    but practiced only compassion toward others,
and bore what must be borne
with a determined heart.

READING THE NEWSPAPER

God our Governor, our Judge, our Peace:
    the pains of the world snag my heart,
    and its turmoils trouble my mind.
There is much I wish to help
    but cannot change.
There is much I grieve in the actions of others
    but cannot control.

I rest this globe in your hands.
I trust it to your will, your justice, and your love.
I cry to you for its people in their distress.
I pledge to do my part, in my time and place,
    to bring your reign near.
I release all I cannot help into your mercy
and into the hands of sisters and brothers
I do not know.

Give me now a quiet mind, a spirit of hope,
and an energy of love
for the work and the rest to which you call me.

Give me the humility to live
gracefully with my limitations,
    but without despair.

DRESSING PRAYER

As I dress this morning, Blessed God,
let me clothe myself in you.
Let my commitment in faith
be the undergirding of everything I do.
Let me put on hope,
always open to the future.
Let me wrap love around me
that it may prompt all my actions.
Let me wear virtue like a coat
against the ill-weather of temptation and evil.
Christ be my shining garment, now and always,
in whose name I pray.

A CHILD'S BREAKFAST GRACE

Thank you for the night that is past.
Bless this breakfast, eaten fast.
Walk with us throughout the day
    and guide our feet in your right way.
Bless us, each, at this day's start.
Guard us, each, while we're apart.
Then, honoring you in all we've done,
    at evening bring us safely home.

SENDING OFF A CHILD
TO SCHOOL

Child of my heart,
 may the blessing of the Holy Trinity
 go with you today.
May the Father's strength keep you secure.
May Christ our true Wisdom guide your learning.
May the Holy Spirit make you glad and good.
May the enfolding of the Trinity
 hold you and bring you, at day's end,
 safely home.

SENDING OFF A LOVED ONE

In the *amen* of the closing door
I commend to your care
this one who is so dear to me.
Through the hours of the day
 be *his* companion;
 guide *his* growth,
 deepen *his* love,
 increase *his* compassion,
 make fruitful *his* work,
 keep *him* in safety,
 and at day's close bring *him* home secure;
through Jesus our Savior.

FOR A CHILD'S TEACHERS

God our Wisdom:
give your blessing and guidance to all who teach,
especially those who teach our child.
I give you thanks for them!
May they, by word and example,
lead all their students
more deeply into the knowledge and love of you
and the appreciation and understanding
     of your world.
Give them empathy and patience,
humor, clarity, and firmness for their work,
and keep all the children safe in their care;
through Jesus Christ our Savior.

A DASHBOARD PRAYER

With care, I take control of this car,
knowing its power to assist my life,
and to endanger me and others.
I give you thanks for the hands which made it,
for the natural resources of your creation
    that fuel it,
and for the privilege to travel so freely
in a world where many must walk.
May I never forget the costs of this convenience,
or my responsibility for its use.
May I travel safely this day in your care.

FAST GRACE FOR FAST FOOD

My lifetime would not be enough
to praise you well, kind God.
Yet, on the run, I give you thanks
for life, for time, for food!

WHILE TRAVELING BY CAR

Vigilant God,
as my body is in motion in this car,
let my heart always be moving toward you.
Focus my attention on the road;
stir me to kindness toward others
and to a spirit of patience in my car,
and in all my movements
through this world.
Help me to remember I have Jesus
as my constant companion on the road.

two

AT HOME AND WORK

CALENDAR PRAYER

God, you sanctify time and history:
I acknowledge you as Sovereign of *my* time.
As I plan my schedule and update my calendar,
help me to set right priorities,
to use my time and talent justly and prudently.
Help me to remember those
who need the gift of my time most,
especially my dear friends and family.
Let me honor my body
with time for rest and play,
and let me honor you
by keeping sabbath time holy.
I ask this through Jesus Christ,
who entered time to redeem it—and me.

AT THE COMPUTER

God, my Wisdom and Discernment,
be with me as I sit down to work.
I thank you for this computer—
for its ingenuity,
for the connections it brings me,
for the knowledge it makes available.
May I always use it well and to your honor,
keeping from too much use,
choosing the good in what I do
and avoiding the evil,
guarding my words to others
that they may be apt and kind.
May I remember that it is the servant,
and you are the Master
and so, use it always as you would desire.

INTERNET PRAYER

From bugs of modem and router,
from worms, viruses, and internet afflictions,
     deliver us, Good Lord.

From spam, pop-ups, and promotions,
from cyberporn, and bogus addresses,
     deliver us, Good Lord.

From voice-messaging chains and menu options,
from buck-passing between service providers and
cable companies,
     deliver us, Good Lord.

From on-hold muzak and advertising,
from stolen cookies and identity thieves,
     deliver us, Good Lord.

Bless us from our booting up
to our shutting down,
and watch over us as our screen-saver fish,
toasters, landscapes, and family photos
morph across our screens,
and until our partial sight dims forever
before your eternal brightness,
everlasting day dawns, and the shadows flee away.

THE BUSTLE OF WORK

God my wisdom and strength:
in the bustle and busy-ness of work,
fill me with your energetic Spirit,
and remind me to pause and recall
that my labor should find favor in your sight,
so that all my work would do you honor,
by helping you renew the face of the earth.

May your Spirit bless and increase
the creativity of my mind,
the effort of my hands,
my collaborations with colleagues,
my consideration of those I serve,
and my gladness for your love and guidance.

Simple Prayers for Complicated Lives

A DIFFICULT DECISION

God of unfolding mystery
and inexhaustible wisdom:
before me lies a difficult decision
in which I ask your help.
Draw me into the depths of prayer to listen
and to speak my heart's desire.
Lend me clarity to know when I must choose,
and patience to let your will take form within me
until that time, without anxiety.
When the moment of decision comes,
guide me to choose well,
and then, in your mercy,
bless my choice.

A BLESSING FOR HOUSECLEANING

Bless to me the cleaning of my house:

Bless the tidying—
    for you uncover all that is hidden in me.

Bless the washing—
    for you also wash away my sin
    and make me clean.

Bless the vacuuming—
    for you invite me not to let matters lie
    that need my action.

Bless the dusting—
    for you desire to remove everything
    that obscures your image in me.

Bless the sweeping and mopping—
  for you persist in loving us
  even when we resist.

Bless the organizing—
  for you set the cosmos in order.

Bless the dishwashing—
  for it is from your hand
  that the household enjoys food.

Bless the putting away of dishes—
  for when I feed others,
  I share in your work of hospitality.

And, because on the seventh day
you rested from all your work—
  bless, afterwards, my sitting down.

OUT OF THIS MUDDLE

Out of this muddle, I cry to you,
God who has ordered the universe,
in whose hands the cosmos is secure.
Guide me to make a right beginning,
to do those things that are most needful,
and to know when to stop and rest.
Grant me humor and a light spirit
in the face of what seems overwhelming.
Make my hands steady at their work,
my heart steady at its prayer,
and let me, in all things,
navigate by love,
for your love's sake.

PRAYER OF SOMEONE BEING BULLIED

Help me, God, against these bullies
    who frighten and embarrass me
    and fill me with worry and dread.
Protect me with your strong presence.
Help me to know and to trust
that there is no shame in asking for help
    against a stronger enemy,
that it is not weakness to walk away
when someone taunts me,
and that it is not my fault that bullies torment me,
for they do so out of their own fear
    and anger and unhappiness.
So, God, after you deliver me from danger,
help them to act better
    and grow out of their meanness.
Make me strong
    with your wise and quiet strength.

HOPE IN CONFLICT

Holy God,
whose Spirit is both my armor of light
and the enlivener of my vulnerable heart:
    strengthen and equip me
    for this hard struggle.
When conflict heats, let me always
keep my eyes and mind on you,
and on the strong and faithful example
of Christ my Savior.
Let all that I do and say
    be according to your will,
    and do you honor.

LAUNDRY PRAYER

Thank you, God my Life and Joy,
for the days of work and leisure
that have brought me this heap of laundry!
Thank you for the members of this household,
for its guests, even for me,
as I clean away the soil of our shared lives.
Let this labor be a small sign to me
of your Spirit at work and play,
constantly renewing the face of the whole earth
and making it shine with your glory.

WRITING CHECKS

God my true treasure:
be with me as I pay my bills.
Help me to hold each creditor in my prayer—
    those who have made and sold
        the things I have bought,
    those who provide services
        that enhance my life,
    and all whose labor joins with mine
        to build the world.
Let me always first honor you by my generosity
to those whose need is greater than my own.
Let this checkbook be a witness
to what I value and believe,
and make me a prudent
and honest steward of all I have;
through Jesus, whose generosity
to me is unbounded.

IN A FINANCIAL MESS

Stand with me, God of wisdom,
in the mess of my finances:
    in my fear of taking charge of the resources
        entrusted to my care;
    in my preference for ignorance
        over honest acknowledgment of the ways
        I use and fail to use my wealth;
    in my anxiety over debt,
    and in all the pressures of my financial life.
Help me to take one step at a time toward
honoring you through my use of money and
honoring others from whom I buy and borrow.
Make me humble to seek counsel,
grateful for my abundance,
prudent with my limited means,
and patient with myself as I seek to be
a better steward of all you have given me.

GARDEN BLESSING

I bless this garden
in the name of the Holy Trinity,
praising God the Creator who gives the growth,
laboring with God the Son
to turn the soil and bring the harvest,
rejoicing in the Spirit
who renews life
and lends the energetic spark to every cell.

May my garden give God glory
in leaf and bud and fruit
and in its fallow season,
and may I tend my soul
as joyfully, constantly, and patiently
as I tend this patch of earth.

Simple Prayers for Complicated Lives

FOR A NEW PET

Creator God, you love all that you have made:
bless this new pet to me and I to *her,*
as joyful companions.
Receive my promise to give *her* faithful care,
to show *her* kindness,
to keep *her* from all cruelty,
to provide what *she* needs for health and comfort,
to be generous with my time and attention,
and to honor *her* as a gift from your hands.
This I pray through your Spirit,
who gives us both life.

FOR A SICK OR INJURED PET

You made the great whale, Holy One,
    for the joy of it,
    and shaped every creature of the earth.
Hear my prayer for my pet *N,* who is *hurt / ill.*
He is your creature,
    a dear companion of my life.
Let only gentle hands touch *him.*
Strengthen life and health in *him.*
Give *him* awareness of my desire
    to comfort and help.
Be with me in my worry and distress,
and keep us both
in the circle of your healing love.

FOR A PET WHO HAS DIED

God, before whom no sparrow falls
without your knowledge:
in grief I return the body
of my pet *N* to the earth.
I give you thanks for the joy of *her* company,
for the time we have shared,
for the affection we have exchanged.
I entrust *her* to your care,
for in the beauty of your imagination
you created all the creatures for your pleasure,
and brought the delight of *N* into my life,
and I know your love never ceases.

PAUSE IN A BUSY LIFE

God my Peace and Refreshment:
in the hubbub and haste of life,
where I feel breathless and spent,
open your stillness before me,
like a walled garden in which I may stroll
or rest beneath shade-giving trees,
breathing the fragrance of blossom,
and sensing the greening
of your Spirit within me.
Draw me into the sweet oasis of your love.

WRAPPING A GIFT

As I wrap this gift,
I commend to you my beloved friend *N,*
to whom I will give it.
I thank you for this friendship,
which reveals your love,
and for showing your face to me
in the face of my friend.
Bless *her* on the occasion of _____.
May *she* know how much I care for *her*
and how much you care for *her.*
Uphold *her* day by day, Blessed One,
and unfold for *her* the gift of yourself.

HOUSE SOUNDS

God our Word and Song:
thank you for the sounds of my house
that bring me joy and rest:
    the whistling kettle
        and the rustling newspaper,
    the purring cat and the percolating coffee,
    the ticking fridge and the chiming clock,
    the chivvying wren by the kitchen window
        and the electric chirp
        of the hummingbird,
    the nodding hum and sigh of the fan,
    the furnace's rumbling burr and flare—
and somewhere,
        under the woodbin on the hearth,
        a cricket's single,
            small, persistent blessing.

three

EVENING

HOMEWORK PRAYER
*(such as might have been prayed
by the young Apostle Paul)*

The homework I should do
I do not do,
while all those things that are more fun
and that I should not do, I do.
And so I ask some help, dear God, from you
to do now, and do well, what I should do
and then be free for all I'd rather do.

WATCHING TELEVISION

As I invite into my home and mind
a stream of images that come
to persuade, to entertain, to sell, and to teach:
God my Wisdom, give me a discerning eye
and attention to what I shall see,
that I may parse its truth,
delight in its virtues,
enjoy its pleasures,
dismiss its deceits,
shun its debasing violence,
and know when to turn it off.

A WAYFARER'S THANKSGIVING

God of unsettling grace:
you call us forward to seek you
in the new places and people
that are your daily gift.
Thank you for the adventure,
for the road,
for the companionship,
and for the settling down at journey's end.
For you are with us always on the way,
and you are our true home.

AT EVENING LAMPLIGHTING

As the darkness of the world closes in,
Blessed One, you are our Light.
Keep this house in peace and safety
through the hours of the night to come.
As lamps fill our home with brightness,
send also the illumination of your Holy Spirit
to enlighten and cheer our hearts.
Grant us tranquil evening hours,
sleep in good conscience,
and a peaceful waking, renewed by your energy;
through Christ our Defender and Daystar.

A CHILD'S BEDTIME PRAYER

As the sunlight fades away,
God, thank you for this closing day:
for air and water, earth and sky,
    and all the human family;
for all I have from you, dear God:
    for home and pets,
    for toys and food.
And if today I've not pleased you,
help me to start tomorrow new.
Help me to be truthful and kind,
a cheerful helper, a trusty friend.
God, be with children of all lands
who need your strong and loving hands.
All those I love who are not here—
keep them safe within your tender care.
Bless all my dear ones, and this night.
Watch over me as I sleep tight.

BLESSING OVER A CHILD ASLEEP

Spirit of Peace, angels of protection,
strong love of this family,
    enfold my child as *he* sleeps.
This night, may *he* rest free of fear;
    may *his* dreams be full of delight;
    may this house be safe and quiet;
    may the peace of the world increase.

Holy Trinity encircle *him.*
Creator who gave *him* life,
    hold *him* always in love.
Jesus, good companion, stay always by *his* side.
Holy Spirit, fill *him* at *his* breathing out
    and *his* breathing in.
Give *him* your peace.

PRAYER OF DARK AND LIGHT

For all that we do not know:
    for the mystery of God,
    for the unfolding of our hope,
    for the meanings that remain hidden,
    for the times of waiting and watching,
    for the moments we reach our limits
        and are called beyond them,
    for the deep structures of our universe
        and its intricate energies moving
        beyond our sight,
    for the ways in which even those
        we love best are mysterious to us,
    for the questions whose answers
        have not come,
    for the suffering with meaning
        we cannot fathom,
    for the silence after all speaking:
        we offer the prayer of darkness.

For all that you reveal to us:
  for the breadth and delight of learning,
  for the flashes of insight and
      leaps of imagination,
  for the moments your holiness breaks in to us,
  for the heat and energy of life,
  for the fire of love between people,
  for the passion to change and
      build up the world,
  for the dance in which all things
      are connected,
  for the lightness of joy in which you visit us,
  for the embers of faithful friendship
      that warm us,
  for the opening door before us
      through which brightness spills:
          we offer the prayer of light.

In you the night and the day are made whole.
In you beginnings and endings touch.
In you the universe holds together.
In you all things are made new.
From you all blessings spring.
To you we offer our thanks and praise.

FOR A MARRIAGE-BED

May your blessing be upon us and upon our bed.
May our bodies always praise you
    by their tenderness.
May the fire of your Spirit
    burn at the heart of our passion
    and warm all our reconciliations.
May your wisdom guide our delight.
May our pleasure teach us gratitude.
May our rest be deep and secure.
May the love we share
    make your love more fully known.
May our gladness in one another
    spill over in kindness toward all your world.
In your name we pray.

SLEEP IN AN EMPTY HOUSE

God of my peace and comfort:
while I sleep in this empty house,
let every room be full of your Holy Spirit.
Let me breathe in your Spirit with every breath
and rest in the assurance of your Presence.
As I hear the creaks and rustles
of the settling house,
let me sense your blessing on it, and on me.
Let me quiet myself in perfect confidence
of your nearness to me.
In the night sounds outside help me hear
the purposeful music of your creation,
busy about its life by night as by day.
And over and through it all,
let me know your watchful and unceasing care.

GLASS HALF-FULL

Thank you for the hidden blessings of this day,
God of the mustard seed
and the yeast in the flour.
Thank you for the near misses and dangers averted,
    for the storms that waned at sea.
Thank you for those who turned away
        from violence at the last minute,
    for those who did not speak their words
        of hate or anger,
        but instead tried another way.
Thank you for those who did not take
        another drink,
    for those who left an anonymous gift
        in amends for hurt,
    for those who made kind allowances
        for strangers,
    for those who suffered inconvenience
        with cheer.

Thank you for the attention of those who
        avoided disaster,
    for the persistence of those working behind
        the scenes for peace,
    for all those who noticed and helped
        in some modest way.
Thank you for the places where war did not rage,
        though it might have done.
Thank you for the alarms sounded in time,
    the crimes prevented,
    the wise actions of many
        for the common good.
And thank you for all the small, invisible
        kindnesses and mendings—
    the gifts of your Spirit
    that have knit together this world,
    even as the news tells us it is unraveling.
Thank you for all the reasons for hope and joy,
    reasons without number.

TO CAST OUT FEAR

Stand watch with us in the hours of this night
to keep us from all harm.
Fill the corners and closets of this home
with the wholesome presence of your Spirit.
Cast out of this place
all influences of the enemy,
and make this a home wholly yours,
a place where we may live and sleep
in quiet confidence that you are always near.
We pray through Jesus, who says to us,
"Peace. Do not fear."

four

BIRTH

FOR A COUPLE LONGING
TO CONCEIVE A CHILD

God of Abraham and Sarah, Jacob and Rachel,
Zechariah and Elizabeth,
you who have heard the cries
of childless people through the ages:
    hear us also, as we long to conceive a child.

Bless the union of our bodies
that they may bring forth the fruit of love
    as accords with your will.
Make our lives fruitful;
surround us with the joy of children—
    and if it may be possible, with our own.

Keep our hearts turned to one another
in our longing, and keep us from despair,
    from blame, from too much anguish.

Help us, in the midst of our deep yearning,
never to forget
    your abundant blessings to us.

We ask all this in the name of Jesus,
    and of Mary, his mother.

FOR A WOMAN SEEKING
TO CONCEIVE A CHILD
THROUGH NEW TECHNOLOGY

Creator of the Universe:
your hospitable Word
called all things into being,
blessed them, and called them good.
You know my desire to join my creative will
with yours in bringing a child into the world.

Thank you for the gifts of science
that give me hope.
Thank you for the gift of my body—
its potential and strength.
Thank you for the resources I may bring
to the birth and nurture of a child.

Lend your skill to those who would assist me
in bringing a child to birth.

Give me courage and patience in my waiting,
a resilient heart to endure difficulty,
and the humility and grace
to give you praise in everything.

Hear my prayer, and answer my request
through the One who taught me to ask boldly,
Jesus your Child.

IN PREGNANCY

God, Lover of souls, Bringer of life:
through the hours of this day,
    bless me and the child I carry.
Build this tiny body within mine
in health and strength.
Let my child swim in your power
and grow in your love—and my own.
Deepen the bond we share with one another,
    deepen tranquility,
    deepen joy.

DURING A PREGNANCY AT RISK

God our refuge and strength,
the child we have conceived is in peril
and we are caught in anxiety.
Bring us all in safety through
this dangerous passage.
Keep us in reverent attention to one another
through all the distractions of this time of waiting.
Quiet our fears.
Watch over our child,
whom you have known from the beginning
and will always hold in your love,
as you hold us.
And when weariness and worry overcome us,
let us rest in you,
who neither slumber nor sleep.

FOR A CHILD WHO
HAS DIED IN THE WOMB

Hear my cry of anguish, God:
for the child I bear in my body has died,
and has carried away all my hope, all my joy.
Uphold me through the sorrowful labor to come
by your powerful arm.
Though you seem far from me, still I beg:
    do not desert me or leave me comfortless.
Help me to trust that this beloved one,
whom you have known in my womb,
will be held in your mercy and memory always.
Let me know that my child,
    who slides from my arms in this world,
will be held secure by your arms in the next,
in that place of reunion and love,
    the country of all the blessed,
    with your Son, Jesus.

NAMING A STILLBORN CHILD

Beloved child,
known to God as you were forming in the womb:
    we name you *N,*
    and bless you in God's name:
        Father, Son, and Holy Spirit.

We now return you to God's hands
and to that eternal life
which you will enjoy in God's company,
and in which we shall know you
in fullness of life in the realm of heaven,
    where there is no separation or loss
    and every tear is wiped away.

FAREWELL PRAYER
FOR A NEWBORN CHILD

Into your hands, God of mystery and compassion,
we entrust this beloved child who has died,
    this tiny body which will not know the
        delight of this world,
    this little person
    whom we had only begun to know.
We offer to you the months of hope
    and expectation,
the labor which has brought sorrow,
the tears which are sanctified by love.

In you there is promise of newness of life.
In you our bodies are raised from death
    and made shining and whole.
In you nothing is lost or wasted.
In you our mourning will be turned to joy.

These things we believe,
even when you feel so far from us.

Into your hands we release this precious child,
whose memory we shall always carry in love.

Christ, bless *her* on *her* way
    and be *her* resurrection
    and our living hope,
        as you have promised.

DELIVERY ROOM PRAYER

God our Father, defend and protect us.
God our Mother, hold us in your perfect strength
    and kindness.
Holy Spirit, breathe with us each birthing breath,
    lend energy to the pushing of our child
        into new life,
    and breathe the first sacred breath
        into tiny lungs.

Let all the hands that receive our child
touch and hold with a secure love.

Light of Christ, shine on this birthing,
    ease and speed it by your grace,
    and keep us all in safety.

THANKSGIVING FOR THE
BIRTH OF A CHILD

God our Father and Mother,
we rejoice to give you thanks and praise
for bringing our child safely to birth.
As we hold *her* in our arms,
hold us all in your everlasting arms.
Bless the life that we shall share
and the love that we shall offer one another.
Give us the grace we need
to nurture and protect this child as *she* grows
into *her* full stature in Christ,
in whose name we offer our glad thanksgiving.

NAMING A NEWBORN CHILD

God our Life and Joy:
you invite us to name and to know
all your creatures
and to love them as you first loved us.
Look upon our child, *N,*
whom we name before you.
We promise *her* our love,
 our compassion, our protection,
 and our patient attention, lifelong.
Give us grace to make you known to our *daughter*
by all that we do and say.
Keep us steady and true,
 brave and merciful,
 joyful and wise for our child,
  as you are for us.

BRINGING A NEW CHILD HOME
FOR THE FIRST TIME

Blessed God,
you love us like a father, like a mother:
bless us now as the parents of this new child *N.*
Bless our home to be a good harbor,
a place of safe dwelling and joyful returning.
Let love be the doorway
through which our child passes.
Bless *his* coming in and *his* going out.
Let your provision be the roof over *his* head,
and our care be the sheltering walls around *him.*
May *his* friends be many
and *his* neighbors be kind.
And may *he* feel your presence in this home,
beginning today and always.

PSALM FOLLOWING
A SIDS DEATH

God, who watches over us
and neither slumbers nor sleeps:
    were you waking when our child
        ceased to breathe?
Were you watching over us then,
    when our lives were broken in the night
        as we slept?
How, then, shall we find forgiveness
for ourselves or for you?

You have said that you do not willingly grieve us
or heap affliction on us,
    that death does not give you pleasure,
        nor do you punish the innocent
            for the sin of others.

Caught in the web of sorrow,
we seek to find hope again,
to cast aside blame and doubt and to go forward,
   trusting that life's goodness and peace
      may return.

Stand with us now.
Be our strong rock and refuge,
   even before our trust is restored,
   even before forgiveness and peace
      come back to us.

Gather into your arms our child,
whom accident has taken from us,
and hold *him* securely until that time
when we shall be reunited
in that place where all tears are wiped away,
   where love is renewed,
      where those who were lost are found again,
         and we are raised up with you in joy.

FOR A CHILD BORN
WITH PHYSICAL CHALLENGES

God our wisdom and strength,
be with us as we welcome this child,
who brings us unknown challenges and blessings.
Help us to be brave and hopeful,
honest with each other in our fears,
kind to each other in our doubts as in our joys,
and loving to this child,
whose experience of life will stretch and teach us.
Surround us and our child
with wise and gentle helpers.
And give us a sense of your near presence
and the possibilities of grace
beyond what we can imagine.
We pray through Jesus Christ,
our companion on the way.

five

PARENTS
AND CHILDREN

FOR THE BIRTHDAY OF
A BELOVED CHILD

God, I give you thanks
for this beloved child *N,*
who is beginning another a year of life.
Lift *her* up in joy,
    guard *her* steps,
    and guide *her* growth.
Grant that the love we have for one another
may give growth to both our souls,
    and deepen our sense
    of your love for each of us.
We ask this through Jesus, your beloved Child.

FOR A SICK CHILD

God our Living Water and Healing Balm:
visit my child in *his* illness with your light.
Remedy suffering, injury, and disease.
Bring *him* comfort of body,
    ease of mind, cheer of spirit,
    and mending, tranquil rest,
that *he* may rise up whole and strong
to give you praise when morning comes.

MY AGGRAVATING CHILD

God of small blessings,
thank you for the aggravation of my child:
    for the marvelous way *he* values
        and demands my attention;
    for *his* skill in winning that attention
        with the shout, the thrown toy,
           the overturned cup;
    for the way *he* prizes my company,
        following me everywhere I go;
    for the bold assertions of *his* will
        as *he* becomes *his* own person day by day;
    for the ways *he* is true to *himself,*
        keeping *his* own schedule and
        communicating *his* desires without deceit;
    for *his* courageous exploration of the world
        with exhausting and patient
           determination.

Lend me your wisdom and patience
    to be a wise guardian of *his* growth,
    to take delight in *his* coming into *himself,*
    to be firm and tolerant, loving and kind,
        even when I feel at the end of my rope.
And when it frays, send me the gift of laughter
to bring us back to the joy of each other.

FOR A CHILD IN SHARED CUSTODY

N, I send you out in love.
Your *father / mother* receives you in love,
and in our love you are always held secure.
May no trouble of your parents bring you fear.
May no quarrel of your parents weigh you down.
May each home of yours
be filled with joy and welcome.
May God watch over your going
and your returning,
and bless you through
the difficult settling in between.
I ask this in Jesus' name.

PRAYER OF A PARENT IN ANGER

Stay my hand, Holy One, from violence
and quiet my voice from its rage.
You have given this child into my care,
but anger has overtaken me
and brought us both into danger.
Help me to step back,
even to walk away,
until I regain my patience.
Quiet my mind.
Slow my breathing.
Remind me of my love
and the littleness of my child,
whose safety is in my hands.
Help me to be worthy of your trust.
Let me breathe in your Holy Spirit
and breathe out compassion for my child,
for your mercy's sake.

PRAYER OF AN
IMPERFECT PARENT

God my Mother, my Father:
I confess that I do not love this child
    as I should.
I am not feeling the warmth
    I think I should feel.
I am not rejoicing
    as others think I should rejoice.
And I am struggling
    to give this little one care.
I am sometimes angry, sometimes ashamed,
and often I wish I could run away and hide.

But you have given me and my child life.
You come to me in the face of my child,
    (had I but eyes to see),
and in my eyes my child will first seek your face.

Be with us.
Let your love grow in us.
Warm my heart and strengthen my will
for this holy work of parenting.
Keep me constant and kind.
Send me the good help of others.
Teach me to find joy in my child,
that my child may also find joy in me.
I ask it in the name of your Child, Jesus.

FOR AN ADOLESCENT SON

God of the summoning fire and protecting cloud,
who calls us always forward:
I praise you for my son, moving into manhood,
even as I grieve and celebrate his changing.
Lend me your wisdom to stand beside him
through the years ahead.
Give me courage to receive the one
he is becoming,
    compassion to see the child still within him,
    patience to weather the collisions with himself
        and with me,
    and joy in his growth at every age.
We pray through the inspiration
of your Spirit of Wisdom
and the grace of your own child, Jesus.

FOR AN ADOLESCENT DAUGHTER

Mothering God:
my daughter stands before me, nearly grown.
I thank you for her.
I would wish to pray that she be protected,
    that she might enjoy youth
        and not hurry to be adult,
    that she keep the sweetness of childhood
        and stay innocent of the world
    —but these are prayers for me!
So I ask that she be strong and wise,
    discerning and brave, steady, joyful, and true.
I pray that you will walk with her
through whatever comes,
lift her up when she stumbles,
and renew her hope and trust when they fade.
Give her a heart generous for others
    but prudent also for herself,
and keep her your person always.

PRAYER OF ADOPTIVE PARENTS

When we open the doors of our hearts
to this child, who comes to us
    in challenge and delight,
    and in great promise,
we open them, God, to you.
Confirm our commitment as a family day by day,
    increase our joy,
    broaden our understanding,
    deepen our love,
through Jesus,
in whom you have adopted all of us
and welcomed us into your household
as your children.

six

ASSAULTS
AND INTRUSIONS

AFTER A RAPE

God, you have made me.
You knew me from before I was born.
Hear me now and have mercy!
My body has become a foreign country,
my life has been broken open and spoiled,
my safety has been shattered
and my strength overcome,
and I am filled with bitterness, rage, and grief.
    Come to my help!

Lift me up in the power of your Spirit.
Mend and cleanse my body
with your Presence.
Defend me, body and soul, by your power,
    that I may fear no enemy,
    that I may not be lost in my anger,
    that in time I may feel whole again.

It is hard to ask anything of you
since when harm came to me, I found no help.
Still, I remember your Child, Jesus,
whose body was broken and pierced.
He called to you even in his abandonment,
and you lifted him from the grave
into newness of life.

In his name, I pray.

AFTER AN ASSAULT

Holy God,
Holy and Mighty,
Holy Immortal One:
    when will you vindicate me
    and set me on my feet?
I call out to you to be my strong tower and ally,
for I have been brought low
and no longer trust in my own strength.
Turn the energy and rage of my helplessness
into determination to act justly and with kindness,
    and not to follow the path of my enemy,
    nor to give myself up to shame
    or to thoughts of vengeance,
but to find my confidence and peace of mind
in your righteousness and wisdom.

FOR ONE'S ATTACKER
(when one is ready)

God, our only Justice and Truth,
I need to release my attacker from my hatred
     into your hands.
His presence in my life is intolerable to me.
May *he* be brought to account
     and kept from doing more harm.
May *he* understand the pain *he* has caused
     and turn to you for forgiveness and mercy.
Help me not to carry *him* in my thoughts,
     in my dreams, or in my memory,
but instead to go forward unburdened
toward the healing which you hold out to me,
     and the renewal of your Holy Spirit.

BLESSING OF A HOUSE
AFTER AN INTRUSION

It is desirable to gather a small group of friends for this rite, and possibly to conclude it with a service of Holy Communion. Water may be blessed to sprinkle the house, and incense or sage and sweetgrass may be burned to cleanse it. Any prayers, as appropriate, may be added.

At the Front Door or Place of Break-in
God our defender and shield:
    make secure this home against all enemies.
Be its strong tower and its gate
to keep safe those who dwell here.
Send your cleansing Spirit to inhabit this place
and make it sound and new.

Give your angels charge over its doorways,
and send your blessing on us
as we go out and come in.
    In Jesus' name we pray.

Blessing the Rooms of the House
God, be our courage and renew our trust.
Bless these rooms
which have grown strange to us,
    and make them home again.
Hallow these walls,
    and make them strong to shelter us.
Hallow the doors and windows that give us light
and entrance, and deliver us from the fear
    that they will again admit enemies.
Hallow the garden and grounds
    that they may refresh us and free us from fear.
Hallow the basement and attic, the corners and
closets, the shadows and seldom-used spaces
    with your quiet, protective Presence.

Guard us waking and sleeping in our home,
and stay close to us in our sleepless hours.

Bless these friends who stand by us,
these neighbors who know our worry
and will help keep watch.
In this world with its dangers, help us to know
that you surround us with a kindly community,
and that your grace strengthens us
to trust and to live in joy and peace again.

Where Possessions Have Been Rifled
Giver of all good gifts:
   everything we enjoy in this world
   passes from hand to hand.
Quiet our sense of violation
and rage at a stranger's presence and touch
of things we hold dear and personal.
Help us to release the memory of this intrusion.
Bless and make safe again this place.
Give us grace to pray for our enemies
even before we may be ready to forgive them.
As Jesus said to his friends in their time of trouble,
"Do not fear. My peace be with you."
Let your peace begin to grow in our hearts,
and renew our trust.

Where Possessions Have Been Stolen
God, our only true Treasure:

all that we have comes from you

and is given us only for a season.
Comfort our hearts in our loss and anger.
Help us to relinquish what is gone,
[especially _____,]
and to take joy in the blessings that remain to us,
using and enjoying all things in your service.

Where There Has Been Vandalism
Justice is in your hands, Holy One:

by your Word all things were set in order.
Quiet our hearts from distress
over the destruction done here.
Relieve our minds of the memories of damage
and the marks of others' greed and anger.
Help us to rebuild and restore
this home and the world
so that we may give you glory,
our God who makes all things new.

Where Blood Has Been Shed
Blessed One, you give us life and breath,
    and all of us return to you.
Touch this place where blood has been shed
with the cleansing of your Presence.
Where there is grief,
    bring your comfort.
Where there is horror,
    bring your calming hand.
Where there is desecration,
    breathe your sanctifying Spirit.
Strengthen us to reclaim this place
as your sacred ground,
our home in which you dwell with us.

Where Someone Has Died
God our true Shelter:
    you hold us all in your wisdom and love.
Send your Spirit to this place
where someone *[whom we love]* has died.

Bless and sanctify this room and this home,
and grant that memories of joy
may drive out memories of pain,
that consolation may grow and grief fade,
and that *N* may feast with the saints in light
in the house of your presence for ever.

　　We pray through Jesus, our Savior.

A Prayer for Renewal (with a sprinkling of holy water)
As the early rains renew the parched ground,
Blessed God, renew and restore this dwelling by
your Presence and power.
Keep it a place of happiness and health,
　　a place of hospitality and rest,
　　a place of companionship and safety
　　for those who live here
　　and for their guests.
Renew and restore also the hearts
of this household
that they may live without anxiety or distress
and find you at home with them,
　　now and always,
　　to bless and keep them,
　　Creator, Word and Holy Spirit.

seven

MIXED BLESSINGS

WEARY IN ONGOING ILLNESS

Holy God,
the healing I had hoped for has not come.
I am weary of being weak and helpless,
tired of pain and of being patient.
In despondency I cry to you,
even though I wonder
whether you hear my prayers.

You are the God who brings forth life
    and continually renews
    the face of the ground.
Yours is the power for healing.
Yours is the love which embraces mortal flesh,
    bears its wounds,
    and dies its death.

Nothing I feel is alien to you.

So, still, I call out for your help:
    let this long illness not defeat me,
    nor deform your image in me.
Let it not damage the person I would be for you
and for those I love.

Stay beside me, do not leave me comfortless.
Let me rest awhile in your peace.

CARING FOR
AGING PARENTS

God of Time and Eternity:
be with me as I care for my parents
    in thankfulness for their care for me
        when I was helpless;
    in my grief for their changes and losses;
    in my fear for the imagined
        but unknown future;
    in my worry for their suffering and anxiety;
    in my frustration for their resistance,
        and my own;
    in my exhaustion when so much
        still needs to be done.

Though they depend on me,
they are not my children,
but need still my honor and respect.

Help me speak to them truly,
　　　listen to them carefully,
　　　and be open to the new ways
　　　　　grace may come to us
　　　through the transformations of age.

FOR A LOVED ONE
WITH MEMORY LOSS

Blessed One, so much do you love us that
you have engraved us on the palm of your hands,
that we might never be lost to you.
Help me as I care for *N,* who is so much changed
from the person *she* once was to me.
In my times of frustration,
lend me humor and a patient spirit.
When sadness comes over me,
let the joy of the love we have shared lift me up.
When I am exhausted, lend me your strength,
and help me know when to let go and rest.
Give me grace to live with the present reality,
to cherish the past,
and never to lose hope for the future,
    for in all our times and changes,
    your love holds us fast.

HELPING PARENTS MOVE
TO ASSISTED LIVING

God, be solid ground under my feet
and wisdom for my heart,
as I help my parents move.
There is wrenching and worry for us all,
    the hard work of moving,
    a farewell to roles, to things and places loved,
    and a need to open ourselves to change.
Help us to trust that we will be met with kindness
by those we do not yet know.
Give my parents grace
to bring their sense of home with them
    and to find friends and welcome ahead.
May they feel the comfort
    of your near presence with them as they go
and may they find unexpected joy
in arriving and settling again.

THANKSGIVING FOR HEALING

I thank you, Divine Physician,
for healing and the return of strength.
Your light drives away the shadow of disease;
    your energy restores flagging spirits;
    and your power mends body and mind.
In all these signs you are known
and for them I praise you in joy.
Let wholeness and vigor abide,
so that I may serve you in gratitude and health.
And let all the earth know your love,
which heals and holds us in peace.

FOR ONE DEPLOYED
IN MILITARY SERVICE

Into your care we place our beloved *N*,
asking you to be *her* tower of safety and strength,
her comfort and refuge in danger.
Watch over *her* wherever *she* goes.
Stand at *her* side in battle.
Keep *her* safe from enemy and accident.
Defend *her,* waking and sleeping.
Bless *her* as *she* travels
and let our love be an anchor and a joy for *her*
through the time we are apart,
and then, return *her* to us in safety.

    We ask this in your Holy Name.

ON THE ANNIVERSARY
OF A SUICIDE

Fold into your mercy, kindly God,
our beloved *N* who took *her* life,
and also remember those of us
who still mourn and love *her.*

In the moments when we might feel
we should have been able to hold *her* in this world
and bring *her* happiness enough to live
(even though it was not in our power),
    help us to forgive ourselves.

In the moments anger rises
at the waste, the hurt, the tearing away,
    make us again tenderhearted
    and compassionate.

In the moments grief floods us,
    be our strong rock, our island of respite.

In all our forgetting,
and always in our remembering,
    bless us with a share of your own loving heart
    shown to us in the generous Spirit of Jesus,
    your own beloved, who died,
    in whom *N* lives again,
        and in whom we shall live again eternally.

IN LONELINESS

I call and there is no answer.
I am weary of my own thoughts,
    my own company,
    of carrying the whole weight of my life alone.
Holy One, come and companion me
in these solitary hours.
Let me trust in your presence,
    in your love.
Teach me contentment of heart
in the company of all the solitary people
whom you have joined together
    into your Body, Blessed Christ,
    whose Spirit dwells in us all.

Simple Prayers for Complicated Lives

A HOPED-FOR LOVE

God, known to me in the fire
and the still, small voice:
> you know how I have invested my heart
> and the love for which I hope
> in this relationship, newly begun.
Give me the wisdom to discern my path,
the patience to let the way unfold,
the courage to see and accept the truth,
> whether it is what I desire or not,
and the grace to love generously and well,
as Jesus my Companion and Guide has taught.

RECONCILIATION
BETWEEN FRIENDS

God, mender of the wounds of the heart:
come quickly to help us now.
We speak in haste and anger;
    we injure one another;
    we harden our hearts and turn away;
    we close our ears and do not listen;
    we forget the love we once knew.
Lend us your compassion, God,
your Spirit of reconciliation,
and turn us again to each other.
Help us understand each other's pain
and desire each other's well-being.
And laying our self-interest aside,
let us see your image in the face of the other,
and seek together your new life.

RETRIEVING THE PROMISES
OF MARRIAGE

God, whose promise is faithful, strong, and sure:
    today it seems our shared life
    is only held together by the memory of love,
    by duct tape and rubber bands.
The future feels uncertain for us
and the resources to cope seem few.
Remind us of the joy with which we started,
the hope in which we married,
and the good we wished for one another then.
Renew our tenderness,
our laughter, and our compassion
    through your abiding presence,
    through the companionship of Jesus,
    and through the spark of your Holy Spirit
        in and between us, now and always.

IN A MARRIAGE CRISIS

God of renewal, everywhere your Holy Spirit
breathes new life into creation.
As I stand among the bones of my marriage,
    be with me in my grief.
Purify my anger,
teach me kindness and compassion,
and strengthen me for a future shaped
    according to your desire.
Teach me how to pray well for my spouse,
how to care faithfully for my family,
and how to honor myself as your beloved child.
Guide me to know
    in which things I should ask forgiveness,
    in which things I should change,
    and in which things I should ask
        for the grace to let go,
    trusting in your goodness
    through Jesus, my Savior.

THANKSGIVING FOR A SPOUSE

In no one else is the joy of your love
brought more clearly to me,
in no one else's eyes
do I see more nearly your kind regard,
blessed God,
and so I give you thanks and praise
for my beloved.
Be beside *him* this day and always,
and let *him* feel your love more fully
through my own.

MARRIAGE THANKSGIVING

Blessed Trinity, One God,
in whose dance of love we participate by our love:
    we give thanks for this marriage,
        rooted and founded in you;
    for each other's faithfulness,
    for the good conversation,
        the trustworthy counsel,
        the comfort of touching,
        the labor well shared.
Help us so to continue to grow in your image,
to practice your hospitality,
and to model your forgiving love,
    that our marriage may build up
    the corner of the world
        in which you have set us,
    and bring joy to others, as it does to us.

Simple Prayers for Complicated Lives

THANKSGIVING FOR AGE

Blessed One, long-companion on my way:
    my bones creak your praise,
    my back (slowly) straightens to do you honor,
    I rise (gradually) from my bed
        to do your will on this day.
If I finish fewer tasks,
    may they be done with greater love.
If I remember fewer things,
    may they be held in greater wisdom.
If I act more slowly,
    may I give life greater attention.

Bless me through the changes
and accidents of time.
Uphold me through the wearing down
and wearing out of my parts.
Give me the gifts of love and good humor
to pass along to others.

Forgive me my frustrations and my fears,
my cussed independence and my pride.
Do not let the complaints of my body
shrink my care for your world.

Lend me grace at every stage and at every age
to enjoy some part of this marvelous gift of life
and always to give you thanks.